Body Management Activities

by Janet A. Wessel and Ellen Curtis-Pierce

Fearon Teacher Aids
Belmont, California

Designed and Illustrated by Rose C. Sheifer

ISBN 0-8224-5352-5

Printed in the United States of America

1. 9 8 7 6 5 4 3 2 1

Contents

Meeting Special Needs of Children

AIMS OF THE PROGRAM

In any class, one or more students may be unable to play and perform basic motor skills effectively. If these students can't play, run, jump, and throw at an early age, they may be slow to develop essential motor skills as well as other basic learnings and social skills—or not develop them at all.

Play is a child's way of learning and integrating skills that will be used throughout life. Through play, children come to understand the world about them. Through play, children learn to move and move to learn. And as children gain play and motor skills, their feelings of self-worth and their positive self-images grow.

Most children learn to play and move through the activities of childhood. They learn by interacting with the environment and with their brothers and sisters and their peers. Handicapped children and other children with special needs often lack the opportunities to play with their peers. These children do not develop play and motor skills on their own. They need a structured, sequential curriculum to interact with their peers, gain feelings of self-worth, and achieve success—and the sooner these children can begin such a program, the better.

This Play and Motor Skills Activities Series presents a program of effective instruction strategies through which all children can achieve success in the general physical education program. It is not a pull-out program (that is, the child is not pulled out for therapy or special tutorial assistance); it is not a fix-it program (that is, the child is not segregated until all deficits are remediated). It is a positive program for each child to succeed in a play-and-motor-skills activity program. It is designed to help you, the teacher, set up sequential curricula, plan each child's instructional program, and teach effectively so that each child progresses toward desired learning outcomes.

Three Major Aims of the Program

1. To enable each child to perform basic play and motor skills at the level of his or her abilities;

2. To help each child use these skills in play and daily living activities to maximize his or her health, growth, and development, as well as joy in movement; and

3. To enhance each child's feelings of self-worth and self-confidence as a learner while moving to learn and learning to move.

BOOKS IN THE SERIES

There are eight books in this Play and Motor Skills Activities Series for preprimary through early primary grades, ages 3–7 years.

1. Locomotor Activities
2. Ball-Handling Activities
3. Stunts and Tumbling Activities
4. Health and Fitness Activities
5. Rhythmic Activities
6. Body Management Activities
7. Play Activities
8. Planning for Teaching

The seven activities books are designed to help teachers of children with handicaps and other special-needs children. Each book provides sequential curricula by skill levels. Each book is complete within its cover: sequential skills and teaching activities, games, action words, and checklists for the class's record of progress in each skill and an Individual Record of Progress (IRP) report.

Book 8, *Planning for Teaching*, is an essential companion to each of the seven activities books because it presents not only the steps for planning a teaching unit and providing for individual differences in each lesson, but it also includes a guide to incorporating social skills into units and lessons and also outlines a Home Activities Program. These two guides are particularly important for children with special needs. Because they often have limited opportunities to interact with their peers, these children need planned, sequential learning experiences to develop socially acceptable behaviors. And because special-needs children also often need extensive practice to retain a skill and generalize its use, a Home Activities Program, planned jointly by parent and teacher, can give them the necessary additional structured learning opportunities.

SEQUENTIAL CURRICULA: SUCCESS BY LEVELS

Each child and the teacher evaluate success. Success is built into the sequential curricula by levels of skills and teaching activities.

Each skill is divided into three levels: rudimentary Skill Level 1 and more refined Skill Levels 2 and 3. Each level is stated in observable behavioral movement terms. The skill levels become performance objectives. Children enter the sequential program at their own performance levels. As they add one small success to another and gain a new skill component or move to a higher skill level, they learn to listen, follow directions, practice, create, and play with others.

Within each skill level, your activities are sequenced, so the child can gain understanding progressively. Within each skill, you provide cues to meet each child's level of understanding and ability. The continuum of teaching cues is

1. verbal cues (action words) with physical assistance or prompts throughout the movement,

2. verbal cues and demonstrations,

3. verbal challenges and problem-solving cues such as "can you?" and

4. introduction of self-initiated learning activities.

GAMES

Game activities are identified for each performance objective by skill level in the seven activity books. At the end of each activity book is an alphabetized description of the games. This list includes the name of each game, formation, directions, equipment, skills involved in playing, and the type of play. Just before the list, you'll find selection criteria and ways to adapt games to different skill levels. Many of the game activities can be used to teach several objectives.

ACTION WORDS

Words for actions (step, look, catch, kick), objects (foot, ball, hand), and concepts (slow, fast, far) are used as verbal cues in teaching. These action words should be matched to the child's level of understanding. They provide a bridge to connect skill activities with other classroom learnings. In the seven activity books, action words are identified for each performance objective by skill level, and an alphabetized list of Action Words is provided at the beginning of each book. As you use this program, add words that are used in other classroom activities and delete those that the children are not ready to understand.

CHECKLISTS: A CHILD'S RECORD OF PROGRESS

In each activity book, you'll also find Individual and Class Records of Progress listing each performance objective. You can use one or both to record the entry performance level and progress of each child. The child's Individual Record of Progress can be used as part of the Individualized Educational Program (IEP). The teacher can record the child's entry performance level and progress on the child's IEP report form or use the end-of-the-year checklist report.

By observing each child performing the skills in class (e.g., during play, during teaching of the skill, or in set-aside time), you can meet the special needs of each child. By using the checklists to record each child's entry level performance of objectives to be taught, you can develop an instructional plan for and evaluate the progress of each child.

Assign each child a learning task (skill component or skill level) based on lesson objectives, and plan lesson activities based on the entry performance level to help the child achieve success. Then use the checklists to record, evaluate, and report each child's progress to the parents. With this record of progress, you can review the teaching-learning activities and can make changes to improve them as necessary.

TEACHING STRATEGY

Direct Instruction

Direct Instruction is coaching on specific tasks at a skill level that allows each child to succeed. A structured and sequential curriculum of essential skills is the primary component of Direct Instruction. As the child progresses in learning, the teacher poses verbal challenges and problem-solving questions such as "can you?" and "show me!" Direct Instruction is based on the premise that success builds success and failure breeds failure.

Adaptive Instruction

Adaptive Instruction is modifying what is taught and how it is taught in order to respond to each child's special needs. Adaptive Instruction helps teachers become more responsive to individual needs. Teaching is based on the child's abilities, on what is to be taught in the lesson, and on what the child is to achieve at the end of instruction. Lesson plans are based on the child's entry performance level on the skills to be taught. Students are monitored during instruction, and the activities are adjusted to each student's needs. Positive reinforcement is provided, and ways to correct the performance or behavior are immediately demonstrated.

Children enter the curriculum at different skill levels, and they learn at different rates. The sequential curriculum helps teachers to individualize the instruction for each child in the class. Thus, the same skill can be taught in a class that includes Betty, who enters at Skill Level 1, and James, who enters at Skill Level 3, because the activities are prescribed for the class or group, but the lesson is planned in order to focus on each child's learning task, and each child is working to achieve his or her own learning task. What is important is that each child master the essential skills at a level of performance that matches his or her abilities, interests, and joy.

Since children learn skills at different rates, you might want to use the following time estimates to allot instructional time for a child to make meaningful progress toward the desired level of performance. One or two skill components can usually be mastered in the instructional time available.

120 minutes	180 minutes	240 minutes	360 minutes
▲	▲	▲	▲
Higher Functioning Faster Learner		Slower Functioning Slower Learner	

Body Management Skills and Activities

INTRODUCTION

Goals for Each Child

1. To demonstrate ability to perform basic body management skills taught in the instructional program;

2. To use body management skills in daily living activities in order to maximize healthy development and joy in movement; and

3. To gain greater feelings of self-worth and self-confidence and to gain greater ability in moving to learn and learning to move.

Body management defines the child's understanding of the moving body and body parts. It bears a clear relationship to body image. Consequently, body management skills are an extremely important curricular component for all movement learnings (i.e., "learning to move and moving to learn"). The body image is the child's focal point for any consistent spatial orientation: locating the self and other objects or people in space and using space effectively.

Laterality (awareness of right and left) and directionality (sense of right and left projected into space along with other directional components such as straight, zigzag, curved, forward, backward, and sideward) are all important body concepts for gaining general mobility and stability as well as acquiring skilled movements. Essential to the acquisition of these learnings is the feedback the child receives in moving the total body or body parts.

Efficient body movement has its roots in awareness of one's moving self, in personal space, and in using general space safely with others. Body management skills are taught in a guided, systematic progression from body awareness (actions, parts, shapes, sizes) to movement in personal and general space. The emphasis is on teaching the child about quantity and quality of different movements, especially through exploratory, creative experiences designed by the child whenever this is a viable option. This book presents three levels of activities for each body management skill in the following order:

1. Body actions
2. Body parts
3. Shapes and sizes
4. Use of space
5. Directions in space

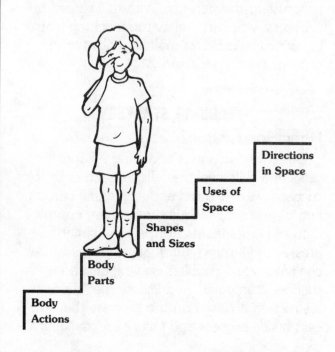

GETTING STARTED

To begin, decide which body management skills you will teach. You can plan a unit or a week or a day or a year. You may decide to teach all skills in this book. Or you may select just a few. Review the checklist for each skill objective you select to teach. Become familiar with the skill components. Next, decide which action words and games you will use in teaching these skills.

Action Words

The words you use are teaching cues. Select ones your children will understand. For each of the body management skills, action words are listed by skill level, and an alphabetized list of words for all the skills in this book is provided below. Circle the words you will use in teaching. If the words you selected prove too difficult for your students, cross them out. Add others that are more appropriate for your children. Star those words that work well.

ACTION	OBJECT	CONCEPT
Bend	Abdominal region	Around
Lie	Ankle	Away from
Move	Arm	Backward
Point	Back	Behind
Raise	Ball	Beside
Reach	Beanbag	Between
Say	Body	Big
Sit	Bottom (seat)	Bottom
Stand	Ceiling	Boundaries
Straighten	Chest	By
Sway	Chin	Curved
Swing	Corners	Down
Touch	Elbow	Far
Turn	Eyes	Forward
Twist	Foot	Front
	Fingers	In
	Floor	In front of
	Hand	Inside
	Head	Large
	Hips	Left
	Jungle gym	Long
	Knee	Look
	Leg	Lower
	Nose	Narrow
	Play area	Near
	Playground	Out
	Playroom	Outside
	Rope	Over
	Scooterboard	Personal
	Seat (bottom)	Ready
	Slide	Right
	Stick	Short
	Stomach	Show me
	Surface (ground)	Sideways
	Swing	Small
	Toes	Space
	Thigh (upper leg)	Straight
	Trunk	Through
	Wall	Top
		Toward
		Under
		Up
		Upper
		Wide
		Width (sides)

Games and Play Activities

In each skill level, you'll find a list of games; select the activity matched to the skills you plan to teach. At the end of this book, you'll find a list of games along with a description of each of them. You'll note that some of the games can be used to teach more than one skill. Use this master list to note those games and play activities that work well and those that do not. Make your comments right on the game listed, or set up a similar format for the games you have selected and make your comments on that sheet. This kind of information can help you plan successful teaching activities.

Equipment

One or more of the following pieces of equipment will be needed for most of the body management activities and games.

1. Chairs
2. Ropes
3. Balls or beanbags
4. Pictures of body parts, actions
5. Colored bands (green and red) for right and left
6. Large boxes
7. Walls or boundary lines
8. Mirrors

Space

Body management activities require enough space for each child to move comfortably and safely. The size of the space depends on the equipment available for the activities and games selected and on the number of children in the class. A multipurpose room with a hardwood floor, and a playground are desirable.

Health and Safety

Space and the equipment should be arranged for safety (mats for landing and falling, handrails or walls for support in climbing stairs). Children with braces, crutches, or wheelchairs may need inclines or a wider base of support or lower step-rise. Children with special visual needs may need a tour of the space and equipment before the lesson. A buddy can be assigned to be near the child when the lesson is taught. Children with special hearing needs may need to be close to the teacher or leader of the activity. The teacher should be positioned to observe all the children during the lesson activities.

Organization: Learning Centers

Learning centers are one of the best types of class organization. You can plan small group learning centers when you know each child's level of performance of the body management skill to be taught. Learning centers can be used to group children by levels of ability or to mix children of different levels of ability. The number of learning centers and their purpose will depend on the number of teachers and support personnel: aides, parent volunteers, older peer models.

To set up a learning center, you should consider the following:

1. **Purpose**	Skills to be taught and practiced
2. **Levels**	Levels 1, 2, and 3, or only one, determined by size of class, space, equipment, support personnel
3. **Grouping**	Same or mixed skill levels
4. **Physical setting**	Location, such as playground or multipurpose room; equipment available; existing physical boundaries, such as walls, or space to make boundaries with chairs, benches, mats, tapes
5. **Activities**	Type of game or instructional activity, such as running on paths, jumping over lines, climbing jungle gym

LEARNING CENTERS: BODY MANAGEMENT ACTIVITIES

LEARNING CENTER 1

Location: classroom

Skill: body parts, body actions, shapes and sizes

Activity: mirror activities, picture card, Do What I Do

Grouping: children at same or different skill levels

LEARNING CENTER 2

Location: multipurpose room

Skill: directions in space, use of space (personal and general)

Activity: move in front of and between chairs, under the table, inside box, touch floor and wall

Grouping: children at same or different skill levels

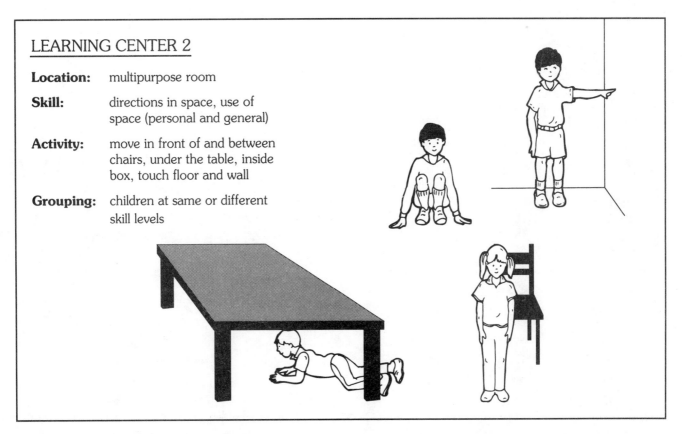

Body Management Activities

BODY ACTIONS: SKILL LEVEL 1

Performance Objective

The child with understanding and ability to move body or body parts can identify body actions by pointing or moving three consecutive times, demonstrating the following skill components:

Within a clear space of 10 feet, the child can

1. bend and straighten trunk (back), elbow, and knee and
2. swing arm and leg and sway total body.

Action Words

Actions: Bend, straighten, sway, swing, turn, twist

Objects: Arm, back, body, elbow, knee, leg, trunk

Concepts: In, left, look, out, ready, right, show me, sideways

Games

- Did You Ever See a Lassie/Laddie?
- Do This, Do That
- Follow the Leader
- Mirror
- Moving Playground
- Obstacle Course
- Simon Says

TEACHING ACTIVITIES

If a child requires assistance to respond,

1. give verbal cues and physical assistance.
Manipulate or guide the child through the entire skill. Face the child in starting position. Put your hands on the child's shoulder and head. Touch the child's head, and push shoulders down close to knees. Push down on waist, hip, and knees so that they are bent and the child is close to the floor. Repeat, bending elbow and knee. Give the child specific verbal instructions throughout (in sign language, bliss symbols, action cues), such as "Bend your body, elbow, and knees."

With the child in a bent position, grasp the child's arms and pull up until he or she is on toes to straighten the total body. Repeat for arm, elbow, and knee. Use verbal cues, such as "Straighten your body (elbow, knee)."

For swaying and swinging, stand at the child's side. Hold the child's hand or wrist, and raise arm forward. Then pull it backward in a swinging motion. Repeat for swinging one leg, having child stand on one leg and manipulating the other leg throughout the swinging action. Then put your hands on the child's upper arm near shoulders. Push on one arm so that child leans to other side, then push on other shoulder until child leans to opposite side. Repeat.

2. give verbal cues with demonstration.
Use a model or have the child watch you bend the total body with waist, hip, and knees bent and body close to floor. Then bend the elbow and knee.

Model the action of straightening the body from a bent position by stretching the body straight up. Then model the bent elbow. Make the correct action of swinging the arms and legs. Emphasize a nonstop pendular motion. Model swaying the whole body and transferring weight from side to side.

After you model the actions of the arm, leg, and the whole body, have the child perform the actions. Use specific verbal instructions (as in 1 above with the modeling).

If a child can respond without assistance,

3. **give a verbal challenge in the form of a problem: "Who can . . . ?" "Show me how you can . . ."**
   a. Bend your body and then straighten your body. Bend your elbow and then straighten your elbow. Bend your knee and then straighten your knee.
   b. Swing your arm and then sway your whole body. Swing your leg and then sway your whole body.
   c. Variation: Bend, straighten; swing, sway to beat of music.

4. **introduce self-initiated learning activities.**
Set up the mats and space for performing body actions. Provide time at the beginning of the lesson and free time for independent learning after the child understands the skills to be used. You may ask the child to create a game activity to play alone or with others (partner or small group) on the carpet squares or mats.

5. **Variations:** Set up an obstacle course that includes colored tape and mats to perform body actions. Play a game, such as Did You Ever See a Lassie/Laddie? Moving Playground, or Simon Says, that incorporates performing body actions.

BODY ACTIONS: SKILL LEVEL 2

Performance Objective

The child with acquisition of Skill Level 1 can identify body actions by pointing or moving three consecutive times, demonstrating the following skill components:

Within a clear space of 10 feet, the child can

3. bend and straighten head, hand, fingers, foot, and toes and

4. twist arm, leg, and trunk, and turn total body and head.

Skills to Review

1. Bend and straighten trunk (back), elbow, and knee and

2. swing arm and leg and sway total body.

Action Words

Actions: Bend, straighten, sway, swing, turn, twist

Objects: Arm, back, body, elbow, fingers, foot, hand, head, knee, leg, toes

Concepts: In, left, look, out, ready, right, show me, sideways

Games

- Did You Ever See a Lassie/Laddie?
- Do This, Do That
- Follow the Leader
- Mirror
- Moving Playground
- Obstacle Course
- Simon Says

TEACHING ACTIVITIES

If a child requires assistance to respond,

1. give verbal cues and physical assistance.
Manipulate or guide the child through the entire skill. Face the child in starting position. Put your hands on the child's shoulder and head. Touch the child's head, and push shoulders down close to knees. Push down so that the child is close to the floor. Repeat, bending elbow and knee. Give the child specific verbal instructions throughout (in sign language, bliss symbols, action cues), such as "Bend your body, elbow, and knees."

With the child in a bent position, grasp the child's arms and pull up until he or she is on toes to straighten the total body. Repeat for arm, elbow, and knee. Use verbal cues, such as "Straighten your body (elbow, knee)," "Tuck."

For swinging, stand at child's side. Hold child's hand or wrist, and raise arm forward. Then pull it backward in a swinging motion. Repeat for swinging one leg.

For twisting, face the child, grasp hand and raise arm in front with elbow straight, then twist arm so that the whole arm twists around, then twist it back to starting position. Repeat with one leg, then the other leg. Use verbal cues, such as "Twist your arm (out, in)."

For turning, face child and place one hand on shoulder and other hand on opposite hip. Pull the shoulder and push the hip to begin the turning motion. Then grasp the other shoulder from the back. Pull on the shoulders, and push the opposite hip to keep the student turning until the motion is complete. Use verbal cues, such as "Turn your whole body." Face child. Place hand on head. Turn child's head to right. Repeat to left.

2. give verbal cues with demonstration.
Use a model or have the child watch you bend and then straighten head, hand, fingers, toes. Gradually reduce the amount of modeling. After modeling, ask child to verbally identify an action. Use specific verbal instructions (as in 1 above with the modeling), such as "Show me how to bend," "What are you doing?" "Bend, straighten." Use same procedure for twist (arms, legs), and turn (whole body, head).

If a child can respond without assistance,

3. give a verbal challenge in the form of a problem: "Who can . . . ?" "Show me how you can . . ." (One cue at a time.)
a. Bend (straighten) your elbow (knee, total body, head, hand, fingers, toes).
b. Swing (sway) your arm (leg, total body).
c. Twist (turn) your arm (leg, total body).
d. Variation: Bend, straighten; swing, sway; twist, turn to beat of music.

4. introduce self-initiated learning activities.
Set up the mats and space for performing body actions. Provide time at the beginning of the lesson and free time for independent learning after the child understands the skills to be used. You may ask the child to create a game activity to play alone or with others (partner or small group) on the carpet squares or mats.

5. Variations: Set up an obstacle course that includes colored tape and mats to perform body actions. Play a game, such as Did You Ever See a Lassie/Laddie? Moving Playground, or Simon Says, that incorporates performing body actions.

BODY ACTIONS: SKILL LEVEL 3

Performance Objective

The child with acquisition of Skill Level 2 or a level of performance appropriate for the child's level of functioning can maintain that level over six weeks.

Given activities that require the skill, the child can

1. play two or more games listed below at home or school, and
2. play with equipment selected by teacher and parent(s).

Skills to Review

1. Level 1 body actions. Bend and straighten trunk (back), elbow, and knee and
2. swing arm and leg and sway total body.
3. Level 2 body actions. Bend and straighten head, hand, fingers, foot, and toes and
4. twist arm, leg, and trunk, and turn total body and head.

Action Words

Actions: Bend, straighten, sway, swing, turn, twist

Objects: Arm, back, body, elbow, fingers, foot, hand, head, knee, leg, toes

Concepts: In, left, look, out, ready, right, show me, sideways

Games

- Did You Ever See a Lassie/Laddie?
- Do This, Do That
- Follow the Leader
- Mirror
- Moving Playground
- Obstacle Course
- Simon Says

TEACHING ACTIVITIES FOR MAINTENANCE

In Teaching

1. Provide the child with teaching cues (verbal and nonverbal, such as demonstration, modeling, imitating) for performing body actions that involve the skill components the child has achieved in compatible teaching and play activities. Bring to the child's attention the skill components he or she has already achieved. Provide positive reinforcement and feedback for the child.
2. Use games that require performing body actions and that involve imitating, modeling, and demonstrating.
3. Observe and assess each child's maintenance at the end of two weeks. Repeat at the end of four weeks (if maintained) and six weeks after initial date of attainment.

▲ Box in the skill level to be maintained on the child's Class Record of Progress. Note the date the child attained target level of performance (defined by teacher alone or co-planned with parents).

▲ Two weeks after attainment, observe the child. Is the level maintained? If child does not demonstrate the skill components at the desired level of performance, indicate the skill components that need reteaching or reinforcing in the comments sheet on the Class Record of Progress. Reschedule teaching time, and co-plan with parents the home activities necessary to reinforce child's achievement of the skill components and maintenance of attainment.

▲ Continue to observe the child, and reteach and reinforce until the child maintains that level of performance for six weeks.

▲ Plan teaching activities incorporating these components so that the child can continually use and reinforce them and can acquire new ones over the year.

▲ When the child can understand it, make a checklist poster illustrating the child's achievements. Bring the child's attention to these skill components in various compatible play and game activities throughout the year. Have the child help others—a partner or a small group.

In Co-Planning with Parent(s)

1. Encourage the parent(s) to reinforce the child's achievement of the skill components in everyday play and living activities in the home.

▲ Provide key action words for the parent(s) to emphasize.

▲ Give the parent(s) a list of play and games to use in playing with the child, thus reinforcing the skill components the child has achieved and needs support to maintain.

▲ Give the parent(s) a list of body action activities that can be emphasized at home with the child, such as

   a. Bending and straightening back, arm, and leg.

   b. Bending and straightening head, hand, fingers, and toes.

   c. Twisting arm, leg, back, and turning body and head.

2. Set up a time every two weeks to interact with the parent(s) and exchange feedback on the child's progress.

BODY PARTS: SKILL LEVEL 1

Performance Objective

The child with understanding and ability to move can identify large body parts by pointing to or moving them three consecutive times, demonstrating the following skill components:

Within a clear space of 10 feet, the child can

1. point to or move large body parts of upper body: head, chest, abdominal region, back, and arm, and

2. point to or move large body parts of lower body: legs, bottom (seat).

Action Words

Actions: Move, point

Objects: Abdominal region, back, bottom (seat), chest, front, head, hips, thigh (upper leg)

Concepts: Large, look, lower, ready, show me, upper

Games

- Body Tag
- Busy Bee
- Did You Ever See a Lassie/Laddie?
- Do This, Do That
- Flash Cards
- Follow the Leader
- Hokey Pokey
- Looby Loo
- Mirror
- Obstacle Course
- Scat
- Simon Says

TEACHING ACTIVITIES

If a child requires assistance to respond,

1. give verbal cues and physical assistance.
Face the child and assist through the entire skill. Move the child's head back and forth, then put the child's hand to head. Repeat with trunk, arms, and legs. Continue manipulating so that the child understands *head, trunk, arms,* and *legs.* Give the child specific verbal instructions throughout (in sign language, bliss symbols, action cues), such as "This is your head," "Move your head (trunk, arms, legs)."

2. give verbal cues with demonstration.
Use a model or have the child watch you move the head, trunk, arms, and legs. Then have the child perform the action. Use specific verbal instructions (as in 1 above with the modeling).

If a child can respond without assistance,

3. **give a verbal challenge in the form of a problem: "Who can . . . ?" "Show me how you can . . ."**
   a. Move your head.
   b. Move your trunk (back).
   c. Move your arms.
   d. Move your legs.
   e. Move your chest.
   f. Move your seat.
   g. Variation: Move body parts to beat of drum.

4. **introduce self-initiated learning activities.**
   Set up mats and space for moving body parts. Provide time at the beginning of the lesson and free time for independent learning after the child understands the skills to be used. You may ask the child to create a game activity to play alone or with others (partner or small group) on the equipment.

5. **Variations:** Set up an obstacle course that includes colored tape and obstacles. Play a game, such as Busy Bee, Flash Cards, or Scat, that incorporates moving body parts.

BODY PARTS: SKILL LEVEL 2

Performance Objective

The child with acquisition of Skill Level 1 can identify three or more small body parts in upper and lower body by pointing to or moving them three consecutive times, demonstrating the following skill components:

Within a clear space of 10 feet, the child can

3. point to or move small body parts of upper body: eyes, ear, face, elbow, hand, and finger, and

4. point to or move small body parts of lower body: knee, foot, heel, ankle, and toe.

Skills to Review

1. Point to or move large body parts of upper body: head, chest, abdominal region, back, and arm and

2. point to or move large body parts of lower body: legs, bottom (seat).

Action Words

Actions: Move, point

Objects: Abdominal region, back, bottom (seat), chest, front, head, hips, thigh (upper leg)

Concepts: Large, look, lower, ready, show me, upper

Games

- Body Tag
- Busy Bee
- Did You Ever See a Lassie/Laddie?
- Do This, Do That
- Flash Cards
- Follow the Leader
- Hokey Pokey
- Looby Loo
- Mirror
- Obstacle Course
- Scat
- Simon Says

TEACHING ACTIVITIES

If a child requires assistance to respond,

1. give verbal cues and physical assistance.
Face the child. Touch the child's nose (chin and eyes). Then take the child's hand, and put it on his or her nose (chin or eyes). Repeat with specified parts of trunk, and arms and legs. Manipulate child to point to or move the correct body part. Give the child specific verbal instructions throughout (in sign language, bliss symbols, action cues), such as "This is your nose (chin, eyes)," "Point to your head," "Move your head," "Show me your head."

2. give verbal cues with demonstration.
Use a model or have the child watch you point to or move the head (nose, chin, seat); arms (elbows, hands, fingers); legs (knees, toes, ankles). Then have child point to or move head, trunk, arms, legs, and small body parts. Use specific verbal instructions (as in 1 above with the modeling).

If a child can respond without assistance,

3. give a verbal challenge in the form of a problem: "Who can . . . ?" "Show me how you can . . ."
a. Show me your nose (chin, eyes).

b. Show me your hips (shoulder, seat, chest, stomach).

c. Show me your elbows (hands, fingers).

d. Show me your legs (feet, heels, toes, ankles).

e. Nod your head.

f. Blink your eyes.

g. Touch your elbow to the wall.

h. Put your hand in the air.

i. Variations: Point to body parts or move to music in singing games.

4. introduce self-initiated learning activities.
Set up the mats and space for moving body parts. Provide time at the beginning of the lesson and free time for independent learning after the child understands the skills to be used. You may ask the child to create a game activity to play alone or with others (partner or small group) on the equipment.

5. Variations: Set up an obstacle course that includes colored tape and obstacles. Play a game such as Busy Bee, Flash Cards, or Scat, that incorporates moving body parts.

BODY PARTS: SKILL LEVEL 3

Performance Objective

The child with acquisition of Skill Level 2 or a level of performance appropriate for the child's level of functioning can maintain that level over six weeks.

Given activities that require the skill, the child can

1. play two or more games, listed below at home or school, and
2. play with equipment selected by teacher and parent(s), including puppetry, picture books, and selected TV programs matched to the skill components.

Skills to Review

1. Level 1 body parts. Point to or move large body parts of upper body: head, chest, abdominal region, back, and arm and
2. point to or move large body parts of lower body: leg, bottom (seat).
3. Level 2 body parts. Point to or move small body parts of upper body: eyes, ear, face, elbow, hand, and finger and
4. point to or move small body parts of lower body: knee, foot, heel, ankle, and toe.

Action Words

Actions: Move, point

Objects: Abdominal region, back, bottom (seat), chest, front, head, hips, thigh (upper leg)

Concepts: Large, look, lower, ready, show me, upper

Games

- Body Tag
- Busy Bee
- Did You Ever See a Lassie/Laddie?
- Do This, Do That
- Flash Cards
- Follow the Leader
- Hokey Pokey
- Looby Loo
- Mirror
- Obstacle Course
- Scat
- Simon Says

TEACHING ACTIVITIES FOR MAINTENANCE

In Teaching

1. Provide the child with teaching cues (verbal and nonverbal, such as demonstration, modeling, imitating) for identifying body parts that involve the skill components the child has achieved in compatible teaching and play activities. Bring to the child's attention the skill components the child has achieved. Provide positive reinforcement and feedback for the child.
2. Use games that require identifying body parts and that involve imitating, modeling, and demonstrating.
3. Observe and assess each child's maintenance at the end of two weeks. Repeat at the end of four weeks (if maintained) and six weeks after initial date of attainment.

▲ Box in the skill level to be maintained on the child's Class Record of Progress. Note the date the child attained target level of performance (defined by teacher alone or co-planned with parents).

▲ Two weeks after attainment, observe the child. Is the level maintained? If child does not demonstrate the skill components at the desired level of performance, indicate the skill components that need reteaching or reinforcing in the comments sheet on the Class Record of Progress. Reschedule teaching time, and co-plan with parents the home activities necessary to reinforce child's achievement of the skill components and maintenance of attainment.

▲ Continue to observe the child, and reteach and reinforce until the child maintains that level of performance for six weeks.

▲ Plan teaching activities incorporating these components so that the child can continually use and

reinforce them and can acquire new ones over the year.

▲ When the child can understand it, make a checklist poster illustrating the child's achievements. Bring the child's attention to these skill components in various compatible play and game activities throughout the year. Have the child help others—a partner or a small group.

In Co-Planning with Parent(s)

1. Encourage the parent(s) to reinforce the child's achievement of the skill components in everyday play and living activities in the home.

▲ Provide key action words for the parent(s) to emphasize.

▲ Give the parent(s) a list of play and games to use in playing with the child, thus reinforcing the skill components the child has achieved and needs support to maintain.

▲ Give the parent(s) a list of body parts that can be emphasized at home with the child, such as

 a. Upper body parts.

 b. Lower body parts.

2. Set up a time every two weeks to interact with the parent(s) and exchange feedback on the child's progress.

SHAPES AND SIZES: SKILL LEVEL 1

Performance Objective

The child with understanding and ability to move body or body parts can move in different shapes and sizes three consecutive times, demonstrating the following skill components:

Within a clear space of 10 feet, the child can

1. move in curved, straight, wide, and narrow shapes and
2. move in large, small, long, and short sizes.

Action Words

Actions: Move, point

Objects: Ankle, arm, back, body, elbow, fingers, foot, hand, knee, leg, toes

Concepts: Curved, large, long, narrow, short, small, straight, wide

Games

- Big and Small
- Did You Ever See a Lassie/Laddie?
- Do This, Do That
- Follow the Leader
- Making Shapes
- Obstacle Course
- Scat
- Simon Says
- Tall and Small

TEACHING ACTIVITIES

If a child requires assistance to respond,

1. give verbal cues and physical assistance.
Manipulate or guide the child through the entire skill. While child is steady, place your hand on shoulders and move them so that back is curved, then straightened. Repeat with arm and leg. Give the child specific verbal instructions throughout (in sign language, bliss symbols, action cues), such as "Make your body (arm, leg) curved," "Make your body straight," "Make your body wide, narrow," "Make your body large, small," "Make your body long, short."

2. give verbal cues with demonstration.
Use a model or have the child watch you make the body or body parts curved or straight (put shoulders back and forward, wide or narrow). Stretch arms and legs as far as possible, extending arms above head and raising up on toes, then kneel, curving back and folding arms around head for large and small; stretch to make it long, bend to make it

short. Then have the child perform the action. Use specific verbal instructions (as in 1 above with the modeling).

If a child can respond without assistance,

3. **give a verbal challenge in the form of a problem: "Who can . . . ?" "Show me how you can . . ."**
   a. Make your body curved (straight), like a line.
   b. Make your body wide (narrow), like paper.
   c. Make your body large (small), like the picture of the elephant or mouse.
   d. Make your body long (short), like lines on floor.
   e. Variations: Make body into different shapes and sizes to beat of the drum.

4. **introduce self-initiated learning activities.**
   Set up the mats and space for moving in shapes and sizes. Provide time at the beginning of the lesson and free time for independent learning after the child understands the skills to be used. You may ask the child to create a game activity to play alone or with others (partner or small group) on the equipment.

5. **Variations:** Set up an obstacle course that includes colored tape and obstacles. Play a game, such as Big and Small, Making Shapes, or Tall and Small, that incorporates moving in shapes and sizes.

SHAPES AND SIZES: SKILL LEVEL 2

Performance Objective

The child with acquisition of Skill Level 1 can move the total body or body parts in contrasting shapes and sizes three consecutive times, demonstrating the following skill components:

Within a clear space of 10 feet, the child can

3. move in contrasting curved-straight and wide-narrow shapes and

4. move in contrasting large-small and long-short sizes.

Skills to Review

1. Move in curved, straight, wide, and narrow shapes and

2. move in large, small, long, and short sizes

Action Words

Actions: Move, point

Objects: Ankle, arm, back, body, elbow, fingers, foot, hand, knee, leg, toes

Concepts: Curved, large, long, narrow, short, small, straight, wide

Games

- Big and Small
- Did You Ever See a Lassie/Laddie?
- Do This, Do That
- Follow the Leader
- Making Shapes
- Obstacle Course
- Scat
- Simon Says
- Tall and Small

TEACHING ACTIVITIES

If a child requires assistance to respond,

1. give verbal cues and physical assistance.
Manipulate or guide the child through the entire skill. While child is steady, place your hand on shoulders and move them so that back is curved, then straightened. Repeat with arm and leg. Give the child specific verbal instructions throughout (in sign language, bliss symbols, action cues), such as "Make your body (arm, leg) curved," "Make your body straight," "Make your body wide, narrow," "Make your body large, small," "Make your body long, short."

2. give verbal cues with demonstration.
Use a model or have the child watch you make body or body parts curved and straight (put shoulders back and forward, wide or narrow). Stretch arms and legs as far as possible, extending arms above head and raising up on toes, then kneel, curving back and folding arms around head for

large and small; stretch to make it long, bend to make it short. Then have the child perform the action. Use specific verbal instructions (as in 1 above with the modeling).

If a child can respond without assistance,

3. **give a verbal challenge in the form of a problem: "Who can . . . ?" "Show me how you can . . ."**
   a. Show me how to make your body (arm, leg) curved or straight. What shape are you making?
   b. Show me how to make your body wide, narrow.
   c. Show me how to make your body large, small.
   d. Show me how to make your body long, short.
   e. Variations: Make your body into different body shapes and sizes to beat of drum.

4. **introduce self-initiated learning activities.** Set up the mats and space for moving in shapes and sizes. Provide time at the beginning of the lesson and free time for independent learning after the child understands the skills to be used. You may ask the child to create a game activity to play alone or with others (partner or small group) on the equipment.

5. **Variations:** Set up an obstacle course that includes colored tape and obstacles. Play a game, such as Big and Small, Making Shapes, or Tall and Small, that incorporates moving in shapes and sizes.

SHAPES AND SIZES: SKILL LEVEL 3

Performance Objective

The child with acquisition of Skill Level 2 or a level of performance appropriate for the child's level of functioning can maintain that level over six weeks.

Given activities that require the skill, the child can

1. play two or more games listed below at home or school, and
2. play with equipment selected by teacher and parent(s), including puppetry, picture books, and selected TV programs matched to the skill components.

Skills to Review

1. Level 1 shapes and sizes. Move in curved, straight, wide, and narrow shapes and
2. move in large, small, long, and short sizes.
3. Level 2 shapes and sizes. Move in contrasting curved-straight and wide-narrow shapes and
4. move in contrasting large-small and long-short sizes.

Action Words

Actions: Move, point

Objects: Ankle, arm, back, body, elbow, fingers, foot, hand, knee, leg, toes

Concepts: Curved, large, long, narrow, short, small, straight, wide

Games

- Big and Small
- Did You Ever See a Lassie/Laddie?
- Do This, Do That
- Follow the Leader
- Making Shapes
- Obstacle Course
- Scat
- Simon Says
- Tall and Small

TEACHING ACTIVITIES FOR MAINTENANCE

In Teaching

1. Provide the child with teaching cues (verbal and nonverbal, such as demonstration, modeling, imitating) for moving in shapes and sizes that involve the skill components the child has achieved in compatible teaching and play activities. Bring to the child's attention the skill components he or she has already achieved. Provide positive reinforcement and feedback for the child.
2. Use games that require moving in shapes and sizes and that involve imitating, modeling, and demonstrating.
3. Observe and assess each child's maintenance at the end of two weeks. Repeat at the end of four weeks (if maintained) and six weeks after initial date of attainment.

▲ Box in the skill level to be maintained on the child's Class Record of Progress. Note the date the child attained target level of performance (defined by teacher alone or co-planned with parents).

▲ Two weeks after attainment, observe the child. Is the level maintained? If child does not demonstrate the skill components at the desired level of performance, indicate the skill components that need reteaching or reinforcing in the comments sheet on the Class Record of Progress. Reschedule teaching time, and co-plan with parents the home activities necessary to reinforce child's achievement of the skill components and maintenance of attainment.

▲ Continue to observe the child, and reteach and reinforce until the child maintains that level of performance for six weeks.

▲ Plan teaching activities incorporating these components so that the child can continually use and reinforce them and can acquire new ones over the year.

▲ When the child can understand it, make a checklist poster illustrating the child's achievements. Bring the child's attention to these skill components in various compatible play and game activities throughout the year. Have the child help others—a partner or a small group.

In Co-Planning with Parent(s)

1. Encourage the parent(s) to reinforce the child's achievement of the skill components in everyday play and living activities in the home.

▲ Provide key action words for the parent(s) to emphasize.

▲ Give the parent(s) a list of play and games to use in playing with the child, thus reinforcing the skill components the child has achieved and needs support to maintain.

▲ Give the parent(s) a list of body shapes and sizes that can be emphasized at home with the child, such as

   a. Curved, straight, wide, narrow.

   b. Large, small, long, short.

   c. Contrasting shapes.

2. Set up a time every two weeks to interact with the parent(s) and exchange feedback on the child's progress.

USE OF SPACE: SKILL LEVEL 1

Performance Objective

The child with understanding and ability to move total body or body parts can identify personal space boundaries by pointing or moving three consecutive times, demonstrating the following skill components:

In assigned personal space area (size depending on safety and class management) the child can

1. identify personal space of top, bottom, width (sides) of body or body movements and

2. identify personal space in play equipment area (sandbox, toys, swing, slide, jungle gym, scooterboard, balls, stick).

Action Words

Actions: Lie, move, point, sit, stand

Objects: Arm, ball, beanbag, body, jungle gym, leg, rope, scooterboard, slide, stick, swing

Concepts: Bottom, boundaries, look, personal, ready, show me, space, top, width (sides)

Games

- Ball in Self Space
- Did You Ever See a Lassie/Laddie?
- Do This, Do That
- Follow the Leader
- My Very Own Space
- Obstacle Course
- Simon Says
- Stretch the Rope

TEACHING ACTIVITIES

If a child requires assistance to respond,

1. give verbal cues and physical assistance.
Manipulate or guide the child through the entire skill. While child is sitting and then standing, stretch child's arms, legs, and head in space around child, top, bottom, and sides. Have child move within 5-by-5-foot square of masking tape. Give the child specific verbal instructions throughout (in sign language, bliss symbols, action cues), such as "Move around in your space," "This is how wide your space is," "Show me the top, bottom of your space," "Show me how wide your space is," "What part of your space is that?"

2. give verbal cues with demonstration.
Use a model or have the child watch you show the boundaries (top, bottom, width, depth) of personal space. Then have the child perform the action. Use specific verbal instructions (as in 1 above with the modeling). Do the same with assigned personal space, using play equipment.

If a child can respond without assistance,

3. give a verbal challenge in the form of a problem: "Who can . . . ?" "Show me how you can . . ."

a. Move the beanbag or base to the top of your space.

b. Move the beanbag or base to the bottom of your space.

c. Move the beanbag or ball to show me how wide your space is.

d. Variations: Use drum, and have child move beanbag to beat of drum in personal space. Use play equipment, and have child move in personal space assigned.

4. introduce self-initiated learning activities.
Set up the mats and space for personal space activities. Provide time at the beginning of the lesson and free time for independent learning after the child understands the skills to be used. You may ask the child to create a game activity to play alone or with others (partner or small group) on the equipment, stressing that the children play together and obey safety rules.

5. Variations: Set up an obstacle course that includes colored tape and obstacles. Play a game, such as Ball in Self Space, My Very Own Space, or Stretch the Rope, that incorporates identifying personal space. Emphasize play equipment that focuses on personal space and safety.

USE OF SPACE: SKILL LEVEL 2

Performance Objective

The child with acquisition of Skill Level 1 can identify general space boundaries by pointing or moving three consecutive times, demonstrating the following skill components:

In general space (emphasis on safety and class rules), the child can

3. identify personal space of walls, corners, ceiling, floor of playroom and
4. identify personal space of sides, surface (ground) of playground area.

Skills to Review

1. Identify personal space of top, bottom, width (sides) of body or body movements and
2. identify personal space in play equipment area (sandbox, toys, swing, slide, jungle gym, scooterboard, balls, stick).

Action Words

Actions: Lie, move, point, sit, stand, touch

Objects: Arm, body, ceiling, corners, floor, leg, play area, playground, playroom, surface (ground), walls

Concepts: Big, bottom, look, ready, show me, space, top, width (sides)

Games

- Do This, Do That
- Follow the Leader
- Obstacle Course
- Simon Says
- Space Walk

TEACHING ACTIVITIES

If a child requires assistance to respond,

1. give verbal cues and physical assistance.
Manipulate or hold the child's shoulders or waist, and guide the child around the general space. Then go to the four walls or boundary lines. Move the child's arm to point to the walls, ceiling, and floor. Give the child specific verbal instructions throughout (in sign language, bliss symbols, action cues), such as "This is everyone's space," "Show me all of the space that belongs to everybody," "Show me the walls, ceilings, floor," "What part of everybody's space is that (point to walls, floor, ceiling)?"

2. give verbal cues with demonstration.
Use a model or have the child watch you point to the boundaries of general space, then move in general space. Emphasize moving to all corners and areas of the space. Then ask the child to perform the action. Use specific verbal instructions (as in 1 above with the modeling).

If a child can respond without assistance,

3. **give a verbal challenge in the form of a problem: "Who can . . . ?" "Show me how you can . . ."**

a. Show me the walls of everybody's space and touch it.

b. Show me the floor or ceiling of everybody's space, touch it or point to it.

c. Move around the boundaries of everybody's space. Point to it and name it.

d. Variations: Use drum and move around space to beat of drum.

4. **introduce self-initiated learning activities.** Set up the equipment and space for general identification activities. Provide time at the beginning of the lesson and free time for independent learning after the child understands the skills to be used. You may ask the child to create a game activity to play alone or with others (partner or small group).

5. **Variations:** Set up an obstacle course that includes colored tape and obstacles. Play a game, such as Space Walk, Simon Says, or Follow the Leader, that incorporates identifying general space. Note: For the playground, modify above for spatial boundaries of the playground area. Emphasize safety rules established for the use of the area.

USE OF SPACE: SKILL LEVEL 3

Performance Objective

The child with acquisition of Skill Level 2 or a level of performance appropriate for the child's level of functioning can maintain that level over six weeks.

Given activities that require the skill, the child can

1. play two or more games listed below at home or school, and
2. play with equipment selected by teacher and parent(s), including community playground equipment and areas, and playroom areas at home or school.

Skills to Review

1. Level 1 space use. Identify personal space of top, bottom, width (sides) of body or body movement and
2. identify personal space in play equipment area (sandbox, toys, swing, slide, jungle gym, scooterboard, balls, stick).
3. Level 2 space use. Identify general space of walls, corners, ceiling, and floor of playroom and
4. identify general space of sides, surface (ground) of playground area.

Action Words

Actions: Lie, move, point, sit, stand, touch

Objects: Arm, ball, beanbag, body, ceiling, corners, floor, jungle gym, leg, play area, playground, playroom, rope, scooterboard, slide, stick, surface (ground), swing, walls

Concepts: Big, bottom, boundaries, look, personal, ready, show me, space, top, width (sides)

Games

- Ball in Self Space
- Did You Ever See a Lassie/Laddie?
- Do This, Do That
- Follow the Leader
- My Very Own Space
- Obstacle Course
- Simon Says
- Space Walk
- Stretch the Rope

TEACHING ACTIVITIES FOR MAINTENANCE

In Teaching

1. Provide the child with teaching cues (verbal and nonverbal, such as demonstration, modeling, imitating) for identifying personal and general space that involve the skill components the child has achieved in compatible teaching and play activities. Bring to the child's attention the skill components he or she has already achieved. Provide positive reinforcement and feedback for the child.
2. Use games that require identifying personal and general space and that involve imitating, modeling, and demonstrating.
3. Observe and assess each child's maintenance at the end of two weeks. Repeat at the end of four weeks (if maintained) and six weeks after initial date of attainment.

▲ Box in the skill level to be maintained on the child's Class Record of Progress. Note the date the child attained target level of performance (defined by teacher alone or co-planned with parents).

▲ Two weeks after attainment, observe the child. Is the level maintained? If child does not demonstrate the skill components at the desired level of performance, indicate the skill components that need reteaching or reinforcing in the comments sheet on the Class Record of Progress. Reschedule teaching time, and co-plan with parents the home activities necessary to reinforce child's achievement of the skill components and maintenance of attainment.

▲ Continue to observe the child, and reteach and reinforce until the child maintains that level of performance for six weeks.

▲ Plan teaching activities incorporating these components so that the child can continually use and

reinforce them and can acquire new ones over the year.

▲ When the child can understand it, make a checklist poster illustrating the child's achievements. Bring the child's attention to these skill components in various compatible play and game activities throughout the year. Have the child help others—a partner or a small group.

In Co-Planning with Parent(s)

1. Encourage the parent(s) to reinforce the child's achievement of the skill components in everyday play and living activities in the home.

▲ Provide key action words for the parent(s) to emphasize.

▲ Give the parent(s) a list of play and games to use in playing with the child, thus reinforcing the skill components the child has achieved and needs support to maintain.

▲ Give the parent(s) a list of activities involving the use of space that can be emphasized at home with the child, such as
   a. Personal space in eating, sitting, standing, sleeping, playing.
   b. General space of playroom or play area, bedroom, home, yard.

2. Set up a time every two weeks to interact with the parent(s) and exchange feedback on the child's progress.

Performance Objective

The child with understanding and ability to move can move the body, arm, or leg in each of the following directions three consecutive times, demonstrating the following skill components:

Within a clear space of 10 feet, the child can

1. move total body, or arm or leg forward, backward, up, and down and
2. move total body, or arm or leg sideways (right, left).

Action Words

Actions: Bend, move, raise, reach, straighten, turn, twist

Objects: Arm, body, leg, rope, wall

Concepts: Backward, down, left, look, ready, right, show me, sideways, up

Games

- Did You Ever See a Lassie/Laddie?
- Discovering Directions
- Do This, Do That
- Follow the Leader
- Let's Pretend
- Obstacle Course
- Right and Left
- Simon Says
- Where Are You?

TEACHING ACTIVITIES

If a child requires assistance to respond,

1. give verbal cues and physical assistance.
Manipulate or guide the child through the entire skill.

a. Face child in standing position. Grasp child's arm, and pull until he or she takes step forward with both feet while body moves forward. Repeat with leg and arm, manipulating the body part forward. Face child, grasp shoulders, and push until child takes step backward with both feet. Repeat with arm and leg, manipulating the body part backward. Give the child specific verbal instructions throughout (in sign language, bliss symbols, action cues), such as "Move your body (arm, leg) forward, backward."

b. Face child in standing position. Hold onto child's hands, and lift them up toward ceiling so that arms are completely extended and the child is steady on toes. Repeat with arm and leg, manipulating until body part is up. With child in standing position, stand in back of child and place your hands on his or her shoulders and push them down. Push down on hips so that waist and knees bend and child is close to floor. Repeat with arm and leg; manipulate body part so that it is down.

c. Face child in standing position. Grasp child's upper arms near shoulders. Push on left shoulder until child steps to right with both feet, moving with whole body to right. Repeat with arm and leg, manipulating the body part to move to the right. Then face the child. Grasp upper arms, push on right shoulder until child steps to left. Use colored armbands to designate direction: green (right), red (left).

d. Give the child specific verbal instructions throughout (in sign language, bliss symbols, action cues), such as "Move your body (arm, leg) to the right," "Move your body to left," "Show me how you can move the body to left, right."

2. give verbal cues with demonstration.
Use a model or have the child watch you move the body (arm, leg) forward and backward. Model the action of moving the body, arm and leg up and down. Model moving to the right or left (be sure to face the same direction as the child). Use specific verbal instructions (as in 1 above with the modeling).

If a child can respond without assistance,

3. give a verbal challenge in the form of a problem: "Who can . . . ?" "Show me how you can . . ."

a. Be a race car and move forward and backward.

b. Be an airplane and move up in the sky and come down to land on the ground.

c. Raise your arm with the green color (right arm). Move in that direction.

d. Move your arm with the red armband. Move in that direction.

e. Variations: Move in various directions (forward, backward; up, down; right, left).

4. introduce self-initiated learning activities.
Set up the mats and space for directional skills activities. Provide time at the beginning of the lesson and free time for independent learning after the child understands the skills to be used.

5. Variations: Set up an obstacle course that includes colored tape and obstacles. Play a game, such as Discovering Directions, Let's Pretend, or Right and Left, that incorporates directional skills.

Performance Objective

The child with acquisition of Skill Level 1 can move the body, arm, or leg in directional-relationship positions to self and objects three consecutive times, demonstrating the following skill components:

Within a clear space of 10 feet, the child can

3. move total body, or arm or leg in front of, behind, beside, between, inside, outside, near, and far and

4. move total body, or arm or leg over (above), under (below), through, around, away from, and toward.

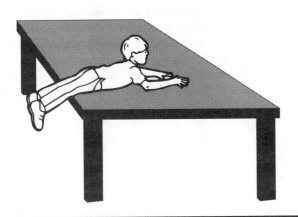
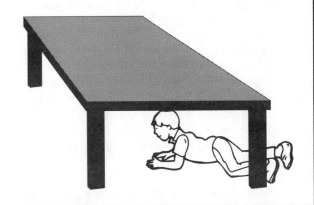

Skills to Review

1. Move total body, or arm or leg forward, backward, up and down and

2. move total body, or arm or leg sideways (right, left).

Action Words

Actions: Bend, move, raise, reach, straighten, sway, turn, twist

Objects: Arm, body, leg, rope, wall

Concepts: Away from *and* toward, backward *and* forward, beside *and* between, far *and* near, in front of *and* behind, inside *and* outside, left *and* right, look, ready, show me, sideways, through *and* around, under *and* over, up *and* down

Games

- Did You Ever See a Lassie/Laddie?
- Discovering Directions
- Do This, Do That
- Follow the Leader
- Let's Pretend
- Obstacle Course
- Right and Left
- Simon Says
- Where Are You?

TEACHING ACTIVITIES

If a child requires assistance to respond,

1. give verbal cues and physical assistance.

a. Face child in standing position. Grasp the child's upper arm by the shoulders. Guide to a position in front of chair. Repeat same manipulation, moving child behind chair. Give the child specific verbal instructions throughout (in sign language, bliss symbols, action cues), such as "Move in front of, behind the chair," "Show me how to move in front of, behind the chair."

b. Face the child. Grasp upper arms by shoulders. Pull child to a position beside chair. Repeat same manipulation to move the child between two chairs. Say, "Move beside, between the chairs," "Show me how to move beside, between the chairs."

c. Face child in standing position. Hold child's hands in yours and keep pulling in direction of wall. Repeat manipulation to move child away from wall. Say, "Move your body toward, away from the wall," "Show me how to move toward, away from the wall."

d. Stand facing the child. Hold the child's hands, and pull him or her to a position next to chair or object. Then pull child to position across the room from the object. Say, "Move your body near, far from the chair," "Show me how to move your body near, far from the chair."

e. Stretch a rope to each side of the room above the level of the child's ankle. Face the child. Pull rope up and over so that the child steps one foot over the rope. Then grasp other ankle and pull it over the rope. Repeat, manipulating the child under the rope by having the child crouch down low. Say, "Move your body over, under the rope," "Show me how to move over, under the rope."

f. Use a large box cut open at both ends. Position child at one end of box. Push down on child's shoulders until he or she is in crouching position. Push on near end of box and then on far end. Then walk with child around the box. Say, "Move your body through, around the box," "Show me how to move through, around the box."

g. Use a box cut open at top. Place it in front of child. Reach down and grasp child's ankle. Lift foot and place it in the box. Repeat, manipulating child outside the box. Say, "Move your body inside, outside the box." "Show me how to move your body inside, outside the box."

2. give verbal cues with demonstration.

a. Use peer model or have child watch you move the body or a body part in front of and behind the chair.

b. Move the body or body parts beside and between the chairs.

c. Move the body or body parts toward and away from the wall.

d. Stand near and far from the object.

e. Move the body, arm, or leg over and under the rope.

f. Move the body, arm, or leg through and then around the box.

g. Place the body, arm, or leg inside and then outside the box.

If a child can respond without assistance,

3. give a verbal challenge in the form of a problem: "Who can . . . ?" "Show me how you can . . ."

a. Move your body in front of the box.

b. Move your body beside the two boxes, or between the two large boxes.

c. Move your body toward, away from the teacher's body.

d. Move your body near, far from the other children in the circle.

e. Move body over, above and under, below the rope.

f. Move body through and around the tunnel.

g. Move body inside, outside of the tires.

4. introduce self-initiated learning activities.
Set up the equipment and space for directional skills activities. Provide time at the beginning of the lesson and free time for independent learning after the child understands the skills to be used.

5. Variations: Set up an obstacle course that includes colored tape and obstacles. Play a game, such as Discovering Directions, Let's Pretend, or Right and Left, that incorporates directional skills.

DIRECTIONS IN SPACE: SKILL LEVEL 3

Performance Objective

The child with acquisition of Skill Level 2 or a level of performance appropriate for the child's level of functioning can maintain that level over six weeks.

Given activities that require the skill, the child can

1. play two or more games listed below at home or school, and
2. play with equipment selected by teacher and parent(s).

Skills to Review

1. Level 1 direction in space. Move total body, or arm or leg forward, backward, up, and down and
2. move total body, or arm or leg sideways (right, left).
3. Level 2 direction in space. Move total body, or arm or leg in front of, behind, beside, between, inside, outside, near, and far and
4. move total body, or arm or leg over (above), under (below), through, around, away from, and toward.

Action Words

Actions: Bend, move, raise, reach, straighten, sway, turn, twist

Objects: Arm, body, leg, rope, wall

Concepts: Away from *and* toward, backward *and* forward, beside *and* between, far *and* near, in front of *and* behind, inside *and* outside, left *and* right, look, ready, show me, sideways, through *and* around, under *and* over, up *and* down

Games

- Did You Ever See a Lassie/Laddie?
- Discovering Directions
- Do This, Do That
- Follow the Leader
- Let's Pretend
- Obstacle Course
- Right and Left
- Simon Says
- Where Are You?

TEACHING ACTIVITIES FOR MAINTENANCE

In Teaching

1. Provide the child with teaching cues (verbal and nonverbal, such as demonstration, modeling, imitating) for directions in space that involve the skill components the child has achieved in compatible teaching and play activities. Bring to the child's attention the skill components he or she has already achieved. Provide positive reinforcement and feedback for the child.

2. Use games that require directions in space and that involve imitating, modeling, and demonstrating.

3. Observe and assess each child's maintenance at the end of two weeks. Repeat at the end of four weeks (if maintained) and six weeks after initial date of attainment.

▲ Box in the skill level to be maintained on the child's Class Record of Progress. Note the date the child attained target level of performance (defined by teacher alone or co-planned with parents).

▲ Two weeks after attainment, observe the child. Is the level maintained? If child does not demonstrate the skill components at the desired level of performance, indicate the skill components that need reteaching or reinforcing in the comments sheet on the Class Record of Progress. Reschedule teaching time, and co-plan with parents the home activities necessary to reinforce child's achievement of the skill components and maintenance of attainment.

▲ Continue to observe the child, and reteach and reinforce until the child maintains that level of performance for six weeks.

▲ Plan teaching activities incorporating these components so that the child can continually use and

reinforce them and can acquire new ones over the year.

▲ When the child can understand it, make a checklist poster illustrating the child's achievements. Bring the child's attention to these skill components in various compatible play and game activities throughout the year. Have the child help others—a partner or a small group.

In Co-Planning with Parent(s)

1. Encourage the parent(s) to reinforce the child's achievement of the skill components in everyday play and living activities in the home.

▲ Provide key action words for the parent(s) to emphasize.

▲ Give the parent(s) a list of play and games to use in playing with the child, thus reinforcing the skill components the child has achieved and needs support to maintain.

▲ Give the parent(s) a list of activities involving spatial directions that can be emphasized at home with the child, such as

   a. Forward, backward, up, down, right, left

   b. In front of, beside, behind, between, inside, outside, near, far

   c. Over, under, through, toward

2. Set up a time every two weeks to interact with the parent(s) and exchange feedback on the child's progress.

Checklists:
Individual and Class Records of Progress

A checklist is an objective score sheet for each body management skill taught in the program. By observing and assessing each child's level of performance, you can identify the activities that will assist the child in reaching the performance objective. Use the same checklist to monitor the child's progress during instruction. When the child's performance level changes, you can upgrade the learning tasks (skill components) to the child's new skill level.

To Begin

Decide on one or more body management activities to be taught in the program. Become familiar with the description of the performance objective for each activity selected. Review the scoring key on the checklist. Plan assessing activities for the selected skills. The number will depend on the class size, the needs of the children, and the help available to you. Set up testing stations similar to the learning stations. Some teachers use free-play time (after setting up equipment for the objective to be tested) to observe the children.

1. Begin assessing at Skill Level 2 for the particular objective. If the child cannot perform at Skill Level 2, assess for Skill Level 1. If the child demonstrates the skill components for Skill Level 2 (i.e., with modeling, verbal cues, or no cues), the child has achieved functional competence. At the next skill level, Skill Level 3, the child demonstrates maintenance retention of the skill over time.

2. For some children with special needs, you may need to assess their levels of functioning before planning teaching activities. As in step 1, observe and assess the amount and type of assistance (cues) the child needs in descending order (i.e., from verbal cues to total manipulation).

Code	Amount and Type of Assistance
SI	Child initiates demonstrating the skill in the teaching and playing of activities
C	Child demonstrates the skill when given verbal cues with or without demonstration
A	Child demonstrates the skill when given partial assistance or total manipulation throughout the execution of the skill

Record, using the code above, the child's initial assistance level and progress in the comments column of the Class Record of Progress. For some children, this may be the most significant initial progress noted (i.e., from assistance to verbal cues and demonstration).

To Assess

1. Be sure all children are working on objectives at other stations while you are assessing at one station.

2. Have two or three children at a testing station ready to be tested together. All other children in the class should be working at other learning stations. On the command "go," each child takes a turn demonstrating knowledge of body management skills. At the end of the trials, the teacher will record the child's performance on the score sheet.

3. You may need to modify the assessing activity by taking a child through the patterns or modeling the activity, or using sign language or an interpreter. Other modifications are individual assessment with no distractions of other children or

activities ongoing in the assessing setting or free play with the equipment. Use mats or movable walls to cut down on distractions.

To Adapt the Checklists

You can note children's skill components adaptations (i.e., physical devices or other changes) in the comments column on the Class Record of Progress. Other changes can be written under recommendations for individual children or the class. Modifications made for a child can be noted on the Individual Record of Progress. The Class Record of Progress can be adapted for an individual child. Record the name of the child rather than the class, and in the name column, record assessment dates. This adaptation may be needed for children whose progress is erratic, because it provides a base line assessment to find out where to begin teaching and evaluating the child's progress.

The Individual Record of Progress for the end-of-the-year report can be attached to the child's IEP (Individual Education Program) report. The record can also serve as a cumulative record for each child. Such records are very useful for new teachers, substitute teachers, aides, and volunteers, as well as parents. The format of the Individual Record of Progress can also be adapted for a Unit Report. The names of all the objectives for a unit—for example, walk-run endurance, running, catching a ball, and rolling a ball—are written rather than the names of the children. Book 8 illustrates the adaptation of the Individual Record of Progress for use in the Home Activities Program and for a Unit Report.

The checklists may be reproduced as needed to implement the play and motor skills program.

CLASS RECORD OF PROGRESS REPORT

CLASS _____   DATE _____

AGE/GRADE _____   TEACHER _____

SCHOOL _____

OBJECTIVE: BODY ACTIONS

SCORING:	SKILL LEVEL 1		SKILL LEVEL 2		SKILL LEVEL 3	PRIMARY RESPONSES:
ASSESSMENT: _____Date **X** = Achieved **O** = Not Achieved **/** = Partially Achieved REASSESSMENT: _____Date **⊗** = Achieved **∅** = Not Achieved	Three Consecutive Times					N = Not Attending NR = No Response UR = Unrelated Response O = Other (Specify in comments)
	Bends and straightens trunk (back), elbow, and knee.	Swings arm and leg and sways total body.	Bends and straightens head, hand, fingers, foot, and toes.	Twists arm, leg, and trunk and turns total body and head.	Two or more play or game activities at home or school demonstrating skill components over six-week period.	
NAME	1	2	3	4	5	COMMENTS
1.						
2.						
3.						
4.						
5.						
6.						
7.						
8.						
9.						
10.						

Recommendations: Specific changes or conditions in planning for instructions, performance, or diagnostic testing procedures or standards. Please describe what worked best.

_____

_____

_____

_____

_____

Class Record of Progress Report

CLASS _____ DATE _____

AGE/GRADE _____ TEACHER _____

SCHOOL _____

Objective: Body Parts

Name	Skill Level 1 — Three Consecutive Times		Skill Level 2		Skill Level 3	Comments
	Points to or moves large body parts of upper body: head, chest, abdominal region, back, and arm.	Points to or moves large body parts of lower body: leg, bottom (seat).	Points to or moves small body parts of upper body: eyes, ear, face, elbow, hand, and finger.	Points to or moves small body parts of lower body: knee, foot, heel, ankle, and toe.	Two or more play or game activities at home or school demonstrating skill components over six-week period.	
	1	2	3	4	5	
1.						
2.						
3.						
4.						
5.						
6.						
7.						
8.						
9.						
10.						

Recommendations: Specific changes or conditions in planning for instructions, performance, or diagnostic testing procedures or standards. Please describe what worked best.

_____

_____

_____

_____

_____

CLASS RECORD OF PROGRESS REPORT

CLASS _____ DATE _____

AGE/GRADE _____ TEACHER _____

SCHOOL _____

OBJECTIVE: SHAPES AND SIZES

SCORING:	SKILL LEVEL 1		SKILL LEVEL 2		SKILL LEVEL 3	PRIMARY RESPONSES:
ASSESSMENT:	Three Consecutive Times					N = Not Attending
_____Date						NR = No Response
X = Achieved						UR = Unrelated Response
O = Not Achieved						
/ = Partially Achieved						O = Other (Specify in comments)
REASSESSMENT:						
_____Date	Moves in curved, straight, wide, and narrow shapes.	Moves in large, small, long, and short sizes.	Moves in contrasting curved-straight and wide-narrow shapes.	Moves in contrasting large-small and long-short sizes.	Two or more play or game activities at home or school demonstrating skill components over six-week period.	
⊗ = Achieved						
Ø = Not Achieved						
NAME	1	2	3	4	5	COMMENTS
1.						
2.						
3.						
4.						
5.						
6.						
7.						
8.						
9.						
10.						

Recommendations: Specific changes or conditions in planning for instructions, performance, or diagnostic testing procedures or standards. Please describe what worked best.

_____

_____

_____

_____

_____

CLASS RECORD OF PROGRESS REPORT

CLASS _____   DATE _____

AGE/GRADE _____   TEACHER _____

SCHOOL _____

OBJECTIVE: USE OF SPACE

SCORING:	SKILL LEVEL 1		SKILL LEVEL 2		SKILL LEVEL 3	PRIMARY RESPONSES:
ASSESSMENT: _____Date **X** = Achieved **O** = Not Achieved / = Partially Achieved REASSESSMENT: _____Date ⊗ = Achieved Ø = Not Achieved	Three Consecutive Times					N = Not Attending NR = No Response UR = Unrelated Response O = Other (Specify in comments)
	Identifies personal space of top, bottom, width (sides) of body or body movement.	Identifies personal space in play equipment area (sandbox, toys, swing, slide, jungle gym, scooterboard, balls, stick).	Identifies general space of walls, corners, ceiling, floor of playroom.	Identifies general space of sides, surface (ground) of playground area.	Two or more play or game activities at home or school demonstrating skill components over six-week period.	
NAME	1	2	3	4	5	COMMENTS
1.						
2.						
3.						
4.						
5.						
6.						
7.						
8.						
9.						
10.						

Recommendations: Specific changes or conditions in planning for instructions, performance, or diagnostic testing procedures or standards. Please describe what worked best.

_____

_____

_____

_____

_____

CLASS RECORD OF PROGRESS REPORT

CLASS _____   DATE _____

AGE/GRADE _____   TEACHER _____

SCHOOL _____

OBJECTIVE: DIRECTIONS IN SPACE

SCORING:

ASSESSMENT:

_____Date

X = Achieved

O = Not Achieved

/ = Partially Achieved

REASSESSMENT:

_____Date

⊘ = Achieved

Ø = Not Achieved

PRIMARY RESPONSES:

N = Not Attending

NR = No Response

UR = Unrelated Response

O = Other (Specify in comments)

NAME	SKILL LEVEL 1 — Three Consecutive Times		SKILL LEVEL 2		SKILL LEVEL 3	COMMENTS
	Moves total body, or arm or leg forward, backward, up, and down.	Moves total body, or arm or leg sideways (right, left).	Moves total body, or arm or leg in front of, behind, beside, between, inside, outside, near, and far.	Moves total body or arm or leg over (above), under (below), through, around, away from, and toward.	Two or more play or game activities at home or school demonstrating skill components over six-week period.	
	1	2	3	4	5	COMMENTS
1.						
2.						
3.						
4.						
5.						
6.						
7.						
8.						
9.						
10.						

Recommendations: Specific changes or conditions in planning for instructions, performance, or diagnostic testing procedures or standards. Please describe what worked best.

_____

_____

_____

_____

_____

INDIVIDUAL RECORD OF PROGRESS

Area: Body Management Skills

CHILD: _____

LEVEL: _____

YEAR: _____

TEACHER: _____

SCHOOL: _____

Marking Period	Date
Fall Conference (white)	from_____to_____
Winter Conference (yellow)	from_____to_____
Spring Conference (pink)	from_____to_____
End-of-Year (cumulative) Report (blue)	from_____to_____

Preprimary Play and Motor Skills Activity Program

The Individual Record of Progress lists all of the objectives in which your child receives instruction during the play and motor skills program. The information reported on your child's Individual Record of Progress shows your child's entry performance and progress for a marking period. The end-of-the-year report represents your child's Individual Education Program (IEP) for the objectives selected and taught during the year.

Each objective is broken into small, measurable steps or skill components. This assists the teacher to assess what your child already knew before teaching began and to determine which step to start teaching first. One of the following symbols is marked by each step or skill component of the objective:

X =   The child already knew how to perform this step before teaching it began.

O =   The child did not know how to perform this step before teaching it began or after instruction of it ended.

⊗ =   The child did not know how to perform this step before teaching it began, but did learn how to do it during the instruction period.

This information should be helpful to you in planning home activities to strengthen your child's play and motor skills.

Comments

_____

_____

_____

_____

_____

_____

_____

_____

_____

BODY ACTIONS

Date: _____

Within a clear space of 10 feet
Three consecutive times

_____ Bends and straightens trunk (back), elbow, and knee.

_____ Swings arm and leg and sways total body.

_____ Bends and straightens head, hand, fingers, foot, and toes.

_____ Twists arm, leg, and trunk and turns total body, and head.

_____ Demonstrates above skill in two or more play or game activities at home or school over a six-week period.

BODY PARTS

Date: _____

Within a clear space of 10 feet
Three consecutive times

_____ Points to or moves large body parts of upper body: head, chest, abdominal region, back, and arm.

_____ Points to or moves large body parts of lower body: leg, bottom (seat).

_____ Points to or moves small body parts of upper body: eyes, ear, face, elbow, hand, and finger.

_____ Points to or moves small body parts of lower body: knee, foot, heel, ankle, and toe.

_____ Demonstrates above skill in two or more play or game activities at home or school over a six-week period.

SHAPES AND SIZES

Date: _____

Within a clear space of 10 feet
Three consecutive times

_____ Moves in curved, straight, wide, and narrow shapes.

_____ Moves in large, small, long, and short sizes.

_____ Moves in contrasting curved-straight and wide-narrow shapes.

_____ Moves in contrasting large-small and long-short sizes.

_____ Demonstrates above skill in two or more play or game activities at home or school over a six-week period.

USE OF SPACE

Date: _____

Three consecutive times

____ Identifies personal space of top, bottom, width (sides) of body or body movement.

____ Identifies personal space in play equipment area (sandbox, toys, swing, slide, jungle gym, scooterboard, balls, stick).

____ Identifies general space of walls, corners, ceiling, floor of playroom.

____ Identifies general space of sides, surface (ground) of playground area.

____ Demonstrates above skill in two or more play or game activities at home or school over a six-week period.

DIRECTIONS IN SPACE

Date: _____

Within a clear space of 10 feet
Three consecutive times

____ Moves total body, or arm or leg forward, backward, up, and down.

____ Moves total body, or arm or leg sideways (right, left).

____ Moves total body, or arm or leg in front of, behind, beside, between, inside, outside, near, and far.

____ Moves total body, or arm or leg over (above), under (below), through, around, away from, and toward.

____ Demonstrates above skill in two or more play or game activities at home or school over a six-week period.

Games

Game Selection

The following game sheets will help you select and plan game activities. They include the names of the games in alphabetical order, formation, directions, equipment, locomotor skills, and type of play activity. Consider the following points when selecting games:

1. Skills and objectives of your program

2. Interest of the child

3. Equipment and rules

4. Adaptability of physical difficulty level in order to match each child's ability

5. Activity for healthy growth and development

6. Social play skill development, such as taking turns, sharing equipment, playing with others, and following and leading

Games can foster creativity. Children enjoy making up, interpreting, and creating their own activities, whether playing alone, with a partner, or with a small group. The time you take to provide opportunities for each child to explore and create will be well spent. One further note. Children can easily create or adapt games matched to their mobility, even if limited by crutches, braces, or wheelchairs. These children easily comprehend how to adapt body management activities with their own expertise for movement.

Following are some suggestions for adapting the physical difficulty level of games and a sequential list of social play development.

Adapting Games

To Change	Use	Example
1. Boundaries	Larger or smaller space	Make Space Walk area larger—from 25 to 50 feet.
2. Equipment	Larger or smaller sizes, weights, or heights, or specially adapted equipment for some children (such as guide-rails, inclines rather than stairs, brightly colored mats)	Use jump ropes of different sizes—2 feet to 6 feet—in stretchy rope.
3. Rules	More or fewer rules	In Scat, touch one or two body parts as directed, then run (jump) to wall.

To Change	Use	Example
4. Actions	More or fewer actions to be performed at one time; play in stationary positions, using various body parts	In Do This, Do That, move two body parts simultaneously.
5. Time of play	Longer or shorter time; frequent rest periods	In Body Type, increase playing time span from 5 minutes to 10 minutes.

To adapt games to other special needs, you might also use buddies and spotters, sign language gestures, or place the child near leader.

Sequential Development of Social Play

Sequence	Description	Example of Play Activity
Individual Play	Child plays alone and independently with toys that are different from those used by other children within speaking distance.	Children explore in own space on carpet. Other children are on carpet, building blocks, playing with cars, etc.
Parallel Play	Child plays independently beside, rather than with, other children.	Child moves ball in own space on rug. Other children also play with balls on rug.
Associate Play	Child plays with other children. There is interaction between children, but there are no common goals.	Child plays Let's Pretend with others, but with no interaction.
Cooperative Play	Child plays within a group organized for playing formal games. Group is goal directed.	Children play Hokey Pokey or Follow the Leader together.

Game Sheet Lesson Plans

Games	Organization	Description/Instructions	Equipment	Skills	Type of Play Activity
Ball in Self Space	Scatter	Have children scatter, each in own space. Say, "This is your very own space. Explore moving body parts in this space." Say, "We can do different things with our balls and in our spaces. Hold onto the ball. Move it high, low, all around. Now lower it and catch it. Throw it up and catch it. Explore the moving ball in your space."	1 ball per child	Personal space	Individual, small group, large group
Big and Small	Large circle	Say, "There are boxes and objects of different shapes and sizes in our circle. This is a large (big) box. Let's walk through large box. But this one is small. We have to make ourselves small to go through small box. Find long line. Walk on long line."	Large, small, wide, and narrow boxes or objects; curved, straight, long, and short lines of tape	Shapes and sizes	Individual, small group, large group
Body Tag	Circle	A child is "it." The child tags any other child on a body part. The tagged child becomes "it." All other children must touch that body part on themselves to avoid being tagged. Emphasize light tap. Repeat action with new "it."	None	Body parts	Small group, large group

Game Sheet Lesson Plans

Games	Organization	Description/Instructions	Equipment	Skills	Type of Play Activity
Busy Bee	Partners, scatter	Partners face each other. Say, "I'm going to name a body part, and you and your partner are going to touch the part I name. Can you and your partner touch hand to hand?" Repeat with head–head, leg–leg, etc. Say to children, "When I say 'Busy Bee,' find a new partner."	None	Body parts	Partners
Did You Ever See a Lassie/Laddie?	Scatter	"Did you ever see a Lassie, a Lassie, a Lassie? Did you ever see a Lassie go this way and that? Go this way and that way, to this way and that? Did you ever see a Lassie go this way and that?" During the song, teacher acts out bending, straightening, swinging, swaying, twisting, turning.	None	Body actions, body parts	Individual, small group, large group
Discovering Directions	Scatter	Children scatter to own space. Say, "Can you move on different parts of your body? I will call a body part, and see if you can move on it. Can you put your stomach on the floor and move forward, backward, sideways, right, left?" Repeat on back on floor, on tiptoes, on all fours, etc.	None	Directions in space	Individual, small group, large group

GAME SHEET LESSON PLANS

GAMES	ORGANIZATION	DESCRIPTION/INSTRUCTIONS	EQUIPMENT	SKILLS	TYPE OF PLAY ACTIVITY
Do This, Do That	Circle × × × × × L × × × ×	Children form circle with leader in middle. Have leader demonstrate a movement such as swinging leg, turning head. Children imitate when leader says "do this." *Do not move when leader says "do that."*	None	Body actions, body parts	Partners, small group, large group
Flash Cards	Scatter × × × × × × × ×	Children scatter. Say, "I'm going to show you a picture of a body part. When you know what the part is, point to that part on your body. Say its name."	Large flash cards with pictures of head, trunk, arm, leg	Body parts	Individual, small group, large group
Follow the Leader	Line × × × ×	Demonstrate various body movements that the child can imitate. Choose different leaders as game progresses.	None	Body actions	Small group, large group

GAME SHEET LESSON PLANS

GAMES	ORGANIZATION	DESCRIPTION/INSTRUCTIONS	EQUIPMENT	SKILLS	TYPE OF PLAY ACTIVITY
Hokey Pokey	Circle	In circle, sing "Hokey Pokey" and do appropriate movements. "Put your arm in, put your arm out, put your arm in and shake it all about. Do the Hokey Pokey and turn yourself around. That's what it's all about." Continue with other body parts.	None	Body parts	Small group
Let's Pretend	Scatter	All children scatter to own space. Say, "Let's pretend to be cars. How do all cars move? Can your car move forward? Can your car move backward? Let's pretend to be airplanes. Do airplanes go up in the air? Can you move body up in air? Go as high as you can—up on tiptoes."	None	Body management	Individual, small group, large group
Looby Loo	Circle	Form circle. Listen to song: "Here we go Looby Loo. Here we go Looby Light. Here we go Looby Loo all on a Saturday night." Children clap hands or move around circle when they hear song. "I put my hand in. I put my hand out. I give my hand a shake, shake, shake, and turn myself about." Continue with arms, elbows, head, and other body parts. Children move appropriate body part.	Looby Loo record	Body parts	Individual, small group, large group

GAME SHEET LESSON PLANS

GAMES	ORGANIZATION	DESCRIPTION/INSTRUCTIONS	EQUIPMENT	SKILLS	TYPE OF PLAY ACTIVITY

Making Shapes	Scatter
	
	X
	X X X
	    X X
	      X
		Say, "We can make different shapes and sizes with our bodies. Can you make your arms and legs curved (demonstrate)? Can you make body long like yard-stick? Short like ruler?"	Objects of different shapes and sizes; slopes; ball; mat; ruler; yardstick	Sizes and shapes	Individual, small group, large group

Mirror	Line [mirror] X X X X	Arrange children in front of mirror. Have them identify body actions and parts in the mirror. Do a movement or point to a specific body part and ask child what it is.	5' x 14' mirror	Body actions, body parts	Partners, small group, large group

GAME SHEET LESSON PLANS

GAMES	ORGANIZATION	DESCRIPTION/INSTRUCTIONS	EQUIPMENT	SKILLS	TYPE OF PLAY ACTIVITY
Moving Playground	Scatter	Say, "Let's think of all the things in playgrounds that swing. Can you make your body swing? When you play softball, the pitcher swings his arm to throw the ball. Can you pretend you are throwing a ball? A tetherball swings; swing like a tetherball." Have children think of things that sway (trees, seesaw, or merry-go-round).	Playground equipment: swings, tetherballs, trees, seesaws	Body actions	Individual, small group, large group
My Very Own Space	Scatter	Children find place and stay there. Say, "This is your very own space. Stay in your space. How big is your space? Show me the top of your space. Where are the sides?" Use body parts to explore space while standing, sitting, lying down.	None	Personal space	Individual, small group, large group

Game Sheet Lesson Plans

Games	Organization	Description/Instructions	Equipment	Skills	Type of Play Activity
Obstacle Course	Scatter X X X X X X X	Set up stations around room. At each station, have cards or people to demonstrate what child must do at station, such as "bend a body part" or "twist your whole body."	None	Body actions	Small group, large group
Right and Left	Scatter X X X X X X X X	All children scatter to own space. Say, "Let's find all the ways to move our bodies forward. Can you move your right arm forward? Your left leg? Your whole body? Can you hop forward, standing on your right foot only? Standing on your toes? Down on all fours?" Have children move on different body parts.	None	Body management	Individual, small group, large group

Game Sheet Lesson Plans

Games	Organization	Description/Instructions	Equipment	Skills	Type of Play Activity
Scat	Lines ten yards ←———— T	Children stand on one line. Say, "When I say 'scat,' run to other line. This time I'm going to try to touch you. Run fast so that I can't touch you. Now listen. Do what I say, and only run when I say 'scat.' Touch your nose, elbows. Scat."	2 lines or tape on floor	Body parts	Small group, large group
Simon Says	Circle X X X X X X X X X X	Say, "When Simon says to do something, do what he says. Ready? Simon says bend your knees. If you don't hear 'Simon says,' don't do anything. Listen carefully. If you moved and I didn't say 'Simon says,' you must sit down for one turn."	None	Body parts	Partner, small group, large group

GAME SHEET LESSON PLANS

GAMES	ORGANIZATION	DESCRIPTION/INSTRUCTIONS	EQUIPMENT	SKILLS	TYPE OF PLAY ACTIVITY
Space Walk	Line, then scatter	Children form line, facing out onto play area. Say, "This is my space in this room. Everybody can move in the big space. This is how big the space is. Here are the walls, the floor, the ceiling. They are called boundaries." Then have children scatter. Say, "Move (walk, run, hop) through all the space, but don't touch anybody. See how many places you can go without touching anyone. Find all the corners."	None (optional: music)	General space	Individual, small group, large group
Stretch the Rope	Scatter	Scatter ropes around room. Have children say, "We can do different things with our ropes and stay in our own space." You say, "Move it to the top of your space. Now to the bottom. Move it to the side. Stretch really far." Explore moving rope in personal space, using different body parts.	1 jump rope (7–8 ft.) per child	Personal space	Individual, small group, large group

Game Sheet Lesson Plans

Games	Organization	Description/Instructions	Equipment	Skills	Type of Play Activity
Tall and Small	Scatter X X X X X X X X	Say, "We are going to learn to make different shapes and sizes with our bodies. Do what I say. 'I am very tall, very tall. I am sometimes tall; I am sometimes small. Guess what I am now.'" Repeat for wide and narrow, large and small, curved and straight, long and short.	None	Directions in space	Individual, small group, large group
Where Are You?	Scatter X X X X X X X X	All children scatter in own space. Say, "Can you move very near to the cone? Very far away from cone? Step over it? Can you put cone behind you? In front of you? Above your head? Beside you?"	1 cone per student	Body management	Individual, small group, large group